D0744211

Hello, Yellow!

by Christianne C. Jones ... illustrated by Todd Ouren

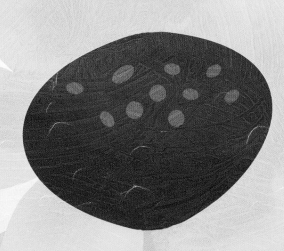

Special thanks to our advisers for their expertise:

Linda Frichtel, Design Adjunct Faculty
Minneapolis College of Art & Design

Susan Kesselring, M.A., Literacy Educator
Rosemount–Apple Valley–Eagan (Minnesota) School District

PICTURE WINDOW BOOKS
Minneapolis, Minnesota

Editor: Jill Kalz
Designer: Amy Muehlenhardt
Page Production: Melissa Kes
Art Director: Nathan Gassman
The illustrations in this book were created digitally.

Picture Window Books
5115 Excelsior Boulevard
Suite 232
Minneapolis, MN 55416
877-845-8392
www.picturewindowbooks.com

37698247 7/08

Printed in the United States of America.

Library of Congress Cataloging-in-Publication Data
Jones, Christianne C.
Hello, yellow! / by Christianne C. Jones ; illustrated by
Todd Ouren.
p. cm. — (Know your colors)
Includes bibliographical references and index.
ISBN-13: 978-1-4048-3111-7 (library binding)
ISBN-10: 1-4048-3111-8 (library binding)
ISBN-13: 978-1-4048-3494-1 (paperback)
ISBN-10: 1-4048-3494-X (paperback)
1. Yellow—Juvenile literature. 2. Color—Juvenile literature.
3. Toy and movable books—Specimens. I. Ouren, Todd, ill.
II. Title.
QC495.5.J658 2007
535.6—dc22   2006027238

The world is filled with COLORS.

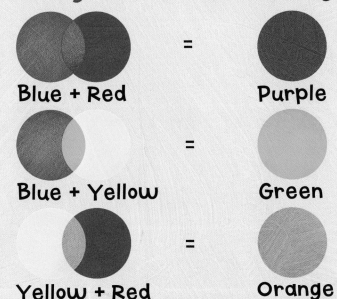

YELLOW
ORANGE
GREEN
RED
BLUE
PURPLE

Colors are either primary or secondary. Red, yellow, and blue are primary colors. These are the colors that can't be made by mixing two other colors together. Orange, purple, and green are secondary colors. Secondary colors are made by mixing together two primary colors.

Black and white are neutral colors. They are used to make other colors lighter or darker.

Primary colors

Blue + Red

Blue + Yellow

Yellow + Red

Secondary colors

=   Purple

=   Green

=   Orange

Keep your eyes open for colorful fun!

3

The color YELLOW makes us happy
from our head to our feet, especially when
a parade comes marching down our street.

4

Tart YELLOW lemonade tastes nice and cold.

Giant **YELLOW** balloons are hard to hold.

8

Shiny YELLOW horns play a song.

Funny YELLOW suits dance along.

13

Chewy YELLOW candy is handed out.

A festive YELLOW float makes us cheer and shout.

The warm YELLOW sun hides in the sky.

19

Bright **YELLOW** gear keeps all of us dry.

The rain falls hard, and the crowd starts to fade.

Can you find more YELLOW at the parade?

MAKE A YELLOW COLLAGE

A collage is a collection of things. It is a work of art. To make one, look around your house and collect yellow items, such as ribbons, glitter, tissue paper, yarn, and pictures from old magazines. Then glue or tape your favorite yellow items to a sheet of yellow construction paper. You've made a yellow collage!

FUN FACTS

- Yellow often stands for hope. In times of war, many people use yellow ribbons to show hope for the soldiers' safe return.

- Yellow is used as a color of warning. A yellow traffic light tells drivers to slow down.

- Some baseballs used to be yellow. In 1938, the Brooklyn Dodgers used yellow baseballs.

- Red, orange, and yellow are called warm colors. Blue, green, and purple are called cool colors.

TO LEARN MORE

AT THE LIBRARY

Anderson, Moira. *Yellow*. Chicago: Raintree, 2006.
Gordon, Sharon. *Yellow*. New York: Benchmark Books, 2005.
Schuette, Sarah L. *Yellow*. Mankato, Minn.: A+ Books, 2003.

ON THE WEB

FactHound offers a safe, fun way to find Web sites related to this book. All of the sites on FactHound have been researched by our staff.

1. Visit *www.facthound.com*
2. Type in this special code: 1404831118
3. Click on the FETCH IT button.

Your trusty FactHound will fetch the best sites for you!

Look for all of the books in the Know Your Colors series:

Autumn Orange

Big Red Farm

Camping in Green

Hello, Yellow!

Purple Pride

Splish, Splash, and Blue

24